Mac

by Murray Ogilvie

Lang**Syne**
PUBLISHING
WRITING *to* REMEMBER

LangSyne

PUBLISHING

WRITING *to* REMEMBER

79 Main Street, Newtongrange,
Midlothian EH22 4NA
Tel: 0131 344 0414   Fax: 0845 075 6085
E-mail: info@lang-syne.co.uk
www.langsyneshop.co.uk

Design by Dorothy Meikle
Printed by Printwell Ltd
© Lang Syne Publishers Ltd 2019

ISBN 978-1-85217-278-7

MacArthur

SEPT NAMES INCLUDE:
Arthur
Dewar
MacCartair
MacCarter
MacIndeor

MacArthur

MOTTO:
Faith and Work.

CREST:
Two laurel wreaths.

TERRITORY:
Argyll.

Chapter one:

The origins of the clan system

by Rennie McOwan

The original Scottish clans of the Highlands and the great families of the Lowlands and Borders were gatherings of families, relatives, allies and neighbours for mutual protection against rivals or invaders.

Scotland experienced invasion from the Vikings, the Romans and English armies from the south. The Norman invasion of what is now England also had an influence on land-holding in Scotland. Some of these invaders stayed on and in time became 'Scottish'.

The word clan derives from the Gaelic language term 'clann', meaning children, and it was first used many centuries ago as communities were formed around tribal lands in glens and mountain fastnesses.

The format of clans changed over the centuries, but at its best the chief and his family held the land on behalf of all, like trustees, and the ordinary clansmen and women believed they had a blood relationship with the founder of their clan.

There were two way duties and obligations. An inadequate chief could be deposed and replaced by someone of greater ability.

Clan people had an immense pride in race. Their relationship with the chief was like adult children to a father and they had a real dignity.

The concept of clanship is very old and a more feudal notion of authority gradually crept in.

Pictland, for instance, was divided into seven principalities ruled by feudal leaders who were the strongest and most charismatic leaders of their particular groups.

By the sixth century the 'British' kingdoms of Strathclyde, Lothian and Celtic Dalriada (Argyll) had emerged and Scotland, as one nation, began to take shape in the time of King Kenneth MacAlpin.

Some chiefs claimed descent from

ancient kings which may not have been accurate in every case.

By the twelfth and thirteenth centuries the clans and families were more strongly brought under the central control of Scottish monarchs.

Lands were awarded and administered more and more under royal favour, yet the power of the area clan chiefs was still very great.

The long wars to ensure Scotland's independence against the expansionist ideas of English monarchs extended the influence of some clans and reduced the lands of others.

Those who supported Scotland's greatest king, Robert the Bruce, were awarded the territories of the families who had opposed his claim to the Scottish throne.

In the Scottish Borders country – the notorious Debatable Lands – the great families built up a ferocious reputation for providing warlike men accustomed to raiding into England and occasionally fighting one another.

Chiefs had the power to dispense justice and to confiscate lands and clan warfare produced a society where martial virtues – courage, hardiness, tenacity – were greatly admired.

Gradually the relationship between the clans and the Crown became strained as Scottish monarchs became more orientated to life in the Lowlands and, on occasion, towards England.

The Highland clans spoke a different language, Gaelic, whereas the language of Lowland Scotland and the court was Scots and in more modern times, English.

Highlanders dressed differently, had different customs, and their wild mountain land sometimes seemed almost foreign to people living in the Lowlands.

It must be emphasised that Gaelic culture was very rich and story-telling, poetry, piping, the clarsach (harp) and other music all flourished and were greatly respected.

Highland culture was different from other parts of Scotland but it was not inferior or less sophisticated.

Central Government, whether in London or Edinburgh, sometimes saw the Gaelic clans as

*"The spirit of the clan means much
to thousands of people"*

a challenge to their authority and some sent expeditions into the Highlands and west to crush the power of the Lords of the Isles.

Nevertheless, when the eighteenth century Jacobite Risings came along the cause of the Stuarts was mainly supported by Highland clans.

The word Jacobite comes from the Latin for James – Jacobus. The Jacobites wanted to restore the exiled Stuarts to the throne of Britain.

The monarchies of Scotland and England became one in 1603 when King James VI of Scotland (1st of England) gained the English throne after Queen Elizabeth died.

The Union of Parliaments of Scotland and England, the Treaty of Union, took place in 1707.

Some Highland clans, of course, and Lowland families opposed the Jacobites and supported the incoming Hanoverians.

After the Jacobite cause finally went down at Culloden in 1746 a kind of ethnic cleansing took place. The power of the chiefs was curtailed. Tartan and the pipes were banned in law.

Many emigrated, some because they

wanted to, some because they were evicted by force. In addition, many Highlanders left for the cities of the south to seek work.

Many of the clan lands became home to sheep and deer shooting estates.

But the warlike traditions of the clans and the great Lowland and Border families lived on, with their descendants fighting bravely for freedom in two world wars.

Remember the men from whence you came, says the Gaelic proverb, and to that could be added the role of many heroic women.

The spirit of the clan, of having roots, whether Highland or Lowland, means much to thousands of people.

*Clan warfare produced a society where
courage and tenacity were greatly admired*

Chapter two:

The rise and fall of the MacArthurs

There are many who believe that the Clan MacArthur is descended from the legendary King Arthur of Round Table fame. Certainly there are several historical arguments which support the notion that Arthur was, if not Scottish, based in Scotland during the sixth century.

Arthur's Seat, an extinct volcano, is in Edinburgh's Old Town. Camelot could have been built there as it is a fine spot for a royal court with uninterrupted views in directions. Merlin's grave is thought to be in a field near the village of Drumelzier close to the River Tweed. Thomas the Rhymer is said to have written the following prophecy: When Tweed and Powsail meet at Merlin's grave, Scotland and England, shall one Monarch have.

This came true in 1603, when the river Tweed overflowed its banks and met the river Powsail at the site of Merlin's Grave – on the very same day that the crowns of Scotland and England were first united under James VI of Scotland who became James I of England. Thomas the Rhymer was a thirteenth century seer, who prophesied in rhyme and was originally known as Thomas of Ercildoune, named after a town in Berwickshire now known as Earlstoun. Thomas is said to have predicted several significant events in Scotland's history including the succession of Robert the Bruce to the throne and the defeat at Flodden. King Arthur died at the Battle of Camlann and that site is thought to be modern-day Camelon near Falkirk.

Some historians believe that the Clan Campbell and Clan Arthur (which later became MacArthur) are both descended from him. However, the first time both families appear in historical records is during the reign (1249-86) of King Alexander III. Their chiefs were MacArthur and MacCailean Mor. The latter, after whom the

Campbells are named, was thought to be the Sheriff of Argyll in the middle of the thirteenth century. Yet, at that time, his kinsmen were not among the landowners of Argyll. Instead, it was the MacArthurs who controlled large estates and were more powerful. And they were to expand their influence still further in the days of Robert the Bruce. After helping him to victory at Bannockburn in 1314, they were rewarded with even more land, taken from the MacDougalls, who had opposed The Bruce. The Clan chief was made Keeper of Dunstaffnage Castle and was handed large parts of the Lorne. The castle, near Oban, had been a MacDougall stronghold until 1309. MacArthur's descendants then extended their control to Strachur on the shores of Loch Fyne along with bits of Glenfalloch and Glendochart, both in Pethshire. This was the best time to be a MacArthur, with the clan at the height of its wealth, power and influence.

But two unconnected events combined to lead to their demise and the ascent of the Clan Campbell. The first was the marriage of Sir Neil

Campbell to Robert the Bruce's sister. There is no question that the Campbells benefited beyond their wildest dreams by marrying into the royal family. Before long they became major landowners and set their sights on the chieftainship of the combined MacArthur-Campbell clan. This was blocked by MacArthur who received a royal charter stating that his lands could only be taken from him by the king. The second major upheaval in the MacArthur fortunes came during the reign of King James I of Scotland (1406-1437). James, who had been born in 1394, had been held prisoner by King Henry IV of England for 18 years, but was freed at the age of 30 and returned home to claim his crown. At that time Scotland was split into lawless factions and James had to take drastic action to regain control. He targeted the clans of the north and west, where allegiance to the crown was transitory. In 1427 he invited many Highland chieftains, including John MacArthur, to a parliament meeting in Inverness. MacArthur was among those the king mistrusted and he was imprisoned and beheaded. His lands were taken from him and from then on the Clan ceased to be a major force in Scotland. The Campbells, meanwhile, continued to grow from strength to strength and eventually were elevated to the Scottish nobility. The MacArthurs held on to some of their land – near Strachur and in bits of Perthshire. And at Dunstaffnage Castle, where they were hereditary keepers, they became tenants of the Campbells.

However, while the ancient MacArthurs suffered a spectacular fall from grace, their more modern descendants certainly did more than their fair share to bring the Clan name back to the fore.

Chapter three:

Controversy and conflict

Douglas MacArthur led a highly controversial life. He became one of America's most famous generals and was responsible for the re-building of Japan after World War Two, but was dismissed from his command at the height of his powers.

He was the grandson of Arthur MacArthur Sr, who was born in Glasgow in 1815, but was taken to the USA as a a teenager when his mother re-married after his father's death. Arthur studied law briefly at college but dropped out to get a job in support of his family during a major depression in 1837. He worked his way up from a legal clerk, first in Boston, then New York and entered the New York bar in 1841. Three years later he married Aurelia Belcher, whose father, a rich industrialist, helped MacArthur establish a lucrative legal practice In Springfield, Massachusetts. However, the relationship between him and his in-laws was strained due to differences in their political beliefs and so MacArthur moved from the east coast to Milwaukee, Wisconsin in 1849. There he quickly gained the friendship and respect of the movers and shakers. Two years later he was elected to the post of City Attorney and in 1855 he accepted the Democratic nomination for lieutenant governor to William A Barstow, who was running for re-election. The election ended in uproar amid accusations of vote rigging. Barstow and MacArthur had won by just 157 votes. Their opponent, Coles Bashford, challenged the result alleging fraud and after an investigation his claim that voting papers were forged was substantiated. Barstow and MacArthur decided to tough it out and were inaugurated on January 7, 1856. But less than three months later, realising the game was up, Barstow resigned. MacArthur became acting governor and despite a rising tide of public opinion against him, and the threat of legal action, he decided to remain in office. However, four days later, he too moved out in favour of Bashford. MacArthur emerged almost unscathed from the episode and was even allowed to remain as lieutenant governor for another year. Indeed, his political career locally and nationally continued smoothly and he was elected twice as a judge in Wisconsin between 1857 and 1869. A year later President Ulysses S Grant appointed him a judge on the Supreme Court of Washington DC, a post he held for 17 years until his retirement. He spent the remainder of his life socialising with the great and good of the nation's capital and became a noted speaker and author, dying in 1896 at the age of 81.

He had two sons. One, Arthur MacArthur Jr, who was born in 1845, became a distinguished general. MacArthur junior studied at the US Military Academy at West Point and when the American Civil War broke out in 1861 he signed up with the 24th Wisconsin Volunteer Infantry. Despite his youth he was a born leader and a brave soldier. His exploits earned him the Medal of Honor, the highest military decoration awarded by the United States. In 1865 he decided to follow his father's footsteps and study law, but it was not for him and within a few months he was back in the army, as a junior officer. For the next 30 years he was posted across the USA, including Little Rock, Arkansas, where Douglas MacArthur was born in 1880. In 1885 Arthur and his family found themselves in New Mexico, where he was involved in the final victory against Geronimo, the famed Apache military leader. MacArthur's first major military action since the Civil War came in the final battle of the Spanish American War, which ended with the USA taking control of former Spanish colonies Guam, The Philippines and Puerto Rico. By now he was a brigadier general and took part in the Battle of Manila. After the Spanish surrender, in August 1898, the Filipinos launched a war of independence against their American occupiers and MacArthur remained there, eventually becoming military governor.

By now his son Douglas was about to begin his own illustrious military career, which would see him join his father in the Philippines.

Chapter four:

The blood is strong

Douglas MacArthur entered West Point in 1899 and graduated as the top student from a class of 930. Like his father his first commission was as a second lieutenant. His first tour of duty, in 1903, was with the third battalion of engineers in the Philippines. It was there that he encountered his first, but certainly not last, brush with death. He was on a surveying mission in the jungle when two armed Filipino insurgents approached him. Without hesitation he drew his pistol and killed them both.

A year later he was back in the USA, as first lieutenant and chief engineering officer for the army's pacific division. That same year he became his father's aide de camp in Tokyo. In 1906 he was fulfilling the same role with President Theodore Roosevelt. After leaving the White House nine months later he, like his father before him, was posted across the country as a military engineer. In 1914, as a captain, he joined the Vera Cruz Expedition as Assistant Engineering Officer. The backdrop for this action was the Mexican revolution. Relations between the USA and its southern neighbour had deteriorated markedly and in an attempt to protect its border America sent a force to blockade the key Mexican port of Vera Cruz. In Mexico MacArthur once again had to fight to save his own life. This time he went on a reconnaissance mission aboard a railway handcar. He was attacked several times by Mexicans but returned to base with nothing more than four bullet holes in his shirt.

It was this disregard for personal danger coupled with his determination to get the job done which marked Douglas MacArthur as an exceptional leader when the Americans entered World War One. This could explain why, in 1917, he was promoted directly two ranks from major to colonel.

During the war he was in charge of the 42nd infantry division, which he formed from units taken from 26 states and the District of Columbia. He nicknamed it the Rainbow Division because he stated that it stretched like a rainbow across the USA. He became the most decorated American serviceman of the war thanks to his bravery and leadership style. He believed in leading from the front and would always be first over the top of trenches, urging his men to follow him into battle. Curiously, he refused to wear a gas mask or hold a weapon. He was twice wounded and suffered breathing problems for the rest of his life. When the war was over he was a brigadier general and had received seven Silver Stars, two Purple Hearts, two Distinguished Service Crosses and a Distinguished Service Medal. He was described by another US general as "The greatest fighting man in the Army".

During the war he criticised the tactics of his commanding officer, General John Pershing, blaming them for the needless loss of American lives. It was the start of a long personal feud between the two. After returning home a hero MacArthur took over the running of West Point. General Pershing, meanwhile, was promoted to army chief of staff and wrote a very negative report of MacArthur's war exploits. Pershing recommended that MacArthur does not receive promotion for several years. But this advice is completely ignored. While many other senior officers were demoted back to their ranks they had prior to the start of the war, MacArthur retained war-time rank and remained a brigadier general. Within five years of Pershing's report he was a major general, which made him the youngest two-star general in the army. It was during this period that Pershing struck again, this time with more serious consequences for MacArthur. In 1922 he married Louise Cromwell Brooks, a vivacious flapper and banking heiress. Pershing, with whom Louise had an affair during the war, sent MacArthur to the Philippines on what was seen by many as a bogus assignment. Although MacArthur was happy to go his new wife was not. She missed the social whirl of New York and the marriage suffered. She eventually sued for divorce in 1928. In the Philippines MacArthur renewed his friendship with the island's leading politician, Manuel Quezon, whom he had known since 1903. The pair had hoped that MacArthur would become governor, but it was not to be. However, President Truman made up for that disappointment by promoting MacArthur to the army's top job, chief of staff in 1930.

About 18 months later, in the summer of 1932, he became embroiled in the most controversial episode of his career.

The Bonus Army was a 17,000-strong group of World war One survivors who, along with their families and other supporters, demonstrated in Washington DC for payments they believed they were owed in return for their war efforts. Unfortunately for them, the certificates with which they were issued eight years earlier did not mature until 1945. The Bonus Army was campaigning for a change of the law which would allow immediate payment to stave off the impact of the economic depression which had gripped the country. The impoverished and destitute old soldiers, along with women and children camped at Anacostia Flats across the river from the Capitol, living in shelters built from packing boxes and scrap tin covered with straw roofs. On June 17 The Senate voted against the bill already passed by Congress to immediately give the Vets their bonus money. A month later the government ordered the removal of the veterans from all government property. But the Vets fought the Washington police, shots were fired and two marchers died. President Hoover ordered in the army under the personal command of Douglas MacArthur, who mobilised units of infantry and cavalry supported by tanks. Early on the evening of July 28 the troops were massed on Pennsylvania Avenue and thousands of Civil Service employees lined the streets to watch. The veterans, thinking the military display was in their honour, cheered. Suddenly soldiers with fixed bayonets, hurling tear gas, charged. That night the Bonus Army retreated into their camp. President Hoover ordered that the army was not to pursue them, because he reckoned it would lead to bad publicity. Twice the order came from the President and twice MacArthur ignored it. His troops chased the Vets into their camp and by early morning it was ablaze. Two babies were killed in the attack and the hospitals were full of wounded victims. MacArthur was convinced that the march was a communist conspiracy to undermine the government, but in this case his instincts were completely wrong and the highly-disturbing sight of the US Army attacking its own people would long linger in the public psyche.

In 1935 MacArthur finished his tour as chief of staff but instead of retiring he remained on the military books as a major general and accepted the job of creating the Philippine Army. In July 1941 he returned to active service as commander of the US forces in the Far East, based in Manila. After the attack on Pearl Harbor, on December 7, 1941, the advancing Japanese chased the Americans out of the Philippines. MacArthur fought a rearguard action but was forced to retreat to Australia, where he planned the fightback. He was awarded the Medal of Honour for his attempts to defend the Philippines and thus created history by becoming the first father and son to win the USA's highest military decoration.

In March 1943 he launched Operation Cartwheel, his strategy to repel the Japanese. It relied heavily on the use of air power and was a resounding success. By the end of 1944 The Philippines had been recaptured and MacArthur began planning the invasion of Japan. However the atom bomb ended Japanese resistance and on September 2, 1945 MacArthur accepted the Emperor's surrender.

From the next three years he was the effective ruler of Japan and oversaw its reconstruction. In 1949 he handed over power to a newly-elected democratic Japanese government, primarily designed by him, but there was no respite from fighting. The Korean war began shortly afterwards and MacArthur assumed command of the UN forces in South Korea. As the Chinese became more involved with helping the north Koreans MacArthur repeatedly asked for permission to attack them inside China. President Truman refused, worried that doing so could lead to nuclear war with the Soviet Union. This infuriated MacArthur, who publicly condemned the President. Eventually, in 1951, Truman dismissed him. It was yet another controversial episode for MacArthur, who returned to the USA and made his final public appearance in a speech to Congress. He was interrupted 30 times by ovations and ended with the famous quote, "Old soldiers never die, they just fade away".

From that point on until his death in 1964, aged 84, MacArthur shunned the limelight and spent time with his family and in the higher echelons of big business. He had re-married in 1937 to Jean Marie Faircloth and they had one child, a son Arthur, who was born a year later. She outlived him by 36 years and died aged 101 in 2000. Such was the public's fascination with Douglas MacArthur that after his death she was often called upon to make speeches about his military career. Three years before he died, MacArthur provided John F Kennedy with a piece of advice which, had it been accepted, would have changed world history. The great general told the young president to avoid a military intervention in Vietnam!

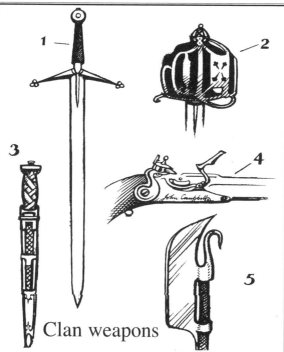

Clan weapons

1) The claymore or two-handed sword *(fifteenth or early six-teenth century)*
2) Basket hilt of broadsword made in Stirling, 1716
3) Highland dirk *(eighteenth century)*
4) Steel pistol *(detail)* made in Doune
5) Head of Lochaber Axe as carried in the '45 and earlier